All The Reasons Why President Trump Should Be Impeached

Copyright 2019. Denise Boland

www.ingramcontent.com/pod-product-compliance
Lightning Source LLC
Chambersburg PA
CBHW041944240526
45473CB00033B/507